AARON SHUST

OOD-BENSON
music publishing
in association with ⓑrash
MUSIC

CONTENTS

Give Me Words

**Words and Music by
AARON SHUST**

Glory to You

Words and Music by
AARON SHUST

8

Matchless

Words and Music by
AARON SHUST

Let the People Praise

Words and Music by
AARON SHUST

Stillness (Speak to Me)

Words and Music by
AARON SHUST

More Wonderful

Words and Music by
AARON SHUST

And al - though it seems at times like it all—— means noth - ing to me,

there.

You got - ta know that I love—— You.

You got - ta know that I need—— You.

You're more won - der - ful.

Give It All Away

Words and Music by
AARON SHUST

Change the Way

Words and Music by
AARON SHUST

My Savior, My God

Words and Music by
AARON SHUST and
MELODY GREENWELL

Stand to Praise (Psalm 117)

Words and Music by
AARON SHUST

In Your Name

Words and Music by
AARON SHUST

In Your name_____ You took_____ the blind_____

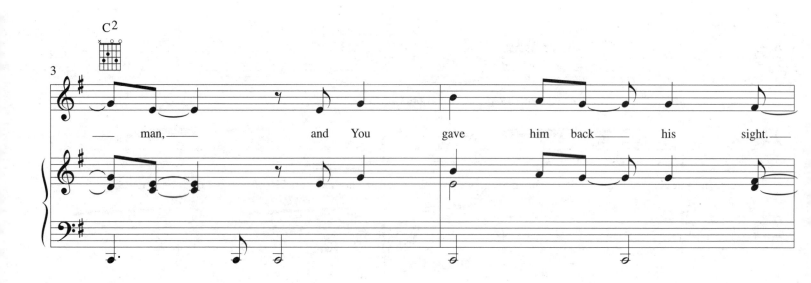

_____ man,_____ and You gave him back_____ his sight._____

In Your name_____ You took_____ the dead

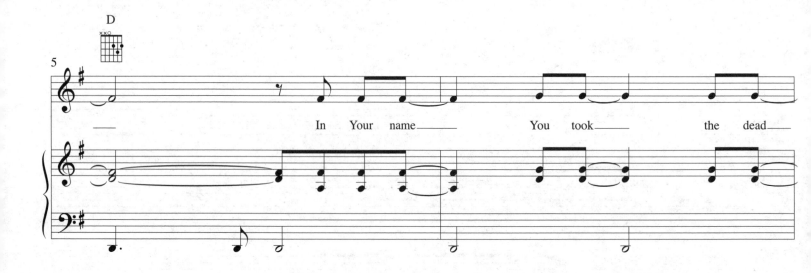

One Day

Words and Music by
AARON SHUST and DAN HANNON

With a strong back beat ♩ = 95

Give Me Words

**Words and Music by
AARON SHUST**

Capo 2 (E)

            E   E/D♯

Give me words to speak; don't let my spirit sleep,

            E/D   Am/C

'Cause I can't think of anything worth saying.

      E   E/D♯   E/D   Am/C

Glory to You

**Words and Music by
AARON SHUST**

Capo 2 (E)

E   E/G#   A   B   E
  Great God of Might, Great God of wonders, Giver of life, Giver of grace.

      E/G#   A   B   A2
Creator of everything before us; You had me in mind before the stars were in place.

     B   E/G# A2   B   E/G# A2
Your love surpasses all by   far. We're praising You for all You   are.

      E
The reason we're here and the reason we sing

     F#m7
Is to thank You, oh God, and give praise to the King.

    C#m7   B   E F#m7 A
We lift up our hands, and we lift up our eyes, and we sing: You are holy.

E   E/G#   A   B   E
  Father of love, Father of mercy, what have I done that You would think about me?

      E/G#   A   B   A2
You've taken my shame; You've taken my sorrow; Replaced them with life and life abundantly.

      E
The reason we're here and the reason we sing

     F#m7
Is to thank You, oh God, and give praise to the King.

    C#m7
We lift up our hearts, and we lift up our minds,

      A   B
And we pray that all we do would bring glory to You.

G A D   G   Bm7   A   D/F#
     You can see inside my heart; You can see inside my mind.

     G   Bm   A
So strip away the things that leave me deaf and blind.

E   E/G#   A   B   A2   F#m7   C#m7   G   D   Bm7   D/F#   Bm

Matchless

Words and Music by
AARON SHUST

G#m   **Emaj7**   **G#m**
   Son of man, Great I AM, King of Heaven, Son of God,
                      Emaj7
You hold the measure of my days.
G#m   **Emaj7**   **G#m**
   Holy Lamb, Spotless Lamb, You are worthy; I am not.
                    Emaj7
Before Your throne I stand amazed.

B   **E2**   **B**   **F#**
   Every tongue confess and every knee will bow
  B/D#   **E2**   **B**   **F#sus**
To Jesus Christ, the Lord forever. Hear our praises now.

           B   **G#m7**   **F#**   **E2**
Your name is matchless. Your name is priceless. Your name means more than I could know.
           B   **G#m7**   **F#**   **E2**
You're so far above me. The way that You love me goes further than any love could go.

G#m   **Emaj7**   **G#m**
   Wonderful Counselor, Root of David, Morning Star,
                    Emaj7
You are the Way, the Truth, the Life.
G#m   **Emaj7**   **G#m**   **Emaj7**
   Lion of the tribe of Judah, Mighty God is who You are, the only perfect sacrifice.

F#   **E2**   **F#**
   In Your name You took the blind man, and You gave him back his sight.
                   E2   **F#**
In Your name You took the dead man, and You brought Him back to life.
                   E2   **F#**
In Your name You took this prisoner, and You opened up the doors,
                   E2
And I will sing before Your throne forevermore.

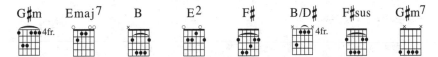

G#m   Emaj7   B   E2   F#   B/D#   F#sus   G#m7

Let the People Praise

Words and Music by
AARON SHUST

G   C   D   G/B   C   D
Our God is the God of gods. And our Lord is the Lord of kings;

Em7   C   G   D/F♯
The revealer of secrets, of mysteries unknown.

C   Dsus   D   G   G/B   C   Dsus   D   G
Let the people praise   our God.   Let the people praise   our God.

Am7   C/D   G   Am7   C/D   G
His sovereign rule will last forever. His kingdom won't decline or fall.

C   C/D   G   D/F♯   Em
He does as He pleases both in heaven and earth.

G/B   C   Am7   Dsus   D
Whom am I that I should question Him at all?

Dsus   G   C
Everything He does is right,   and all His ways are just.

Dsus   G   C
Those who walk in pride He is able to humble.

Dsus   G   C
Everything He does is right,   and all His ways are just.

Dsus   G   C   Dsus   D
Those who walk in pride He is able to humble.

Am7   C/D   G   Am7   C/D   G
He lifts up kings and brings them low again. He shows us what is right from wrong.

C   C/D   G   D/F♯
God of all time, we give You thanks and praise,

Em   G/B   C   Am7   Dsus   D
For   You have made us wise, and You have made us strong.

G   C   D   G/B   Em7   D/F♯   Dsus   Am7   C/D   Em

Stillness (Speak to Me)

**Words and Music by
AARON SHUST**

Capo 1 (G)

G   **D/F♯**   **Em**   **C**
I come to You, oh God, in the stillness of my heart.
G   **D/F♯**   **Em**   **C**
I need Your healing and Your voice in the stillness of my heart.

   G   **G/B**
So, speak to me and show me who You are.
Em   **C**
Rescue me with Your unfailing love and mercy.
Em   **D/F♯**
Speak to me and show me who You are.
C   **D/G** **G** **D/C** **C**
Hold me tightly in Your arms and never let me   go.

G   **D/F♯**   **Em**   **C**
I hear You calling out my name in the stillness of my heart.
G   **D/F♯**   **Em**   **C**
Your grace is given me again, now I open up my heart.

Am7   **C**   **G**
I remember singing praises to Your name
   G/F♯   **Em**
Every day with all my might.
G/A   **Cmaj7**
How I long to sing to You again.

More Wonderful

Words and Music by
AARON SHUST

Gm7(4)   **F2/A**   **B♭2(no3)**
God of unending grace, I come to You on my face.
              Csus   **Gm7(4)**
I need to hear You speak to me. Won't You make me new right now?
              F2/A   **B♭2(no3)**
God of omnipotent power, visit us in this hour.
              Csus
And may we leave here changed because we've met with You, God.

F   **B♭maj9**   **Dm7**   **Csus**
You've been more wonderful to me than I could have ever imagined.
F   **B♭maj9**   **Dm7**   **Csus**
You've shown more love than I could show in a thousand years.
B♭2   **Csus**   **C**   **F**   **C/E**
    And although it seems at times like it all means nothing to me,
Dm   **Dm/C**   **B♭2**   **Csus**   **C**
You gotta know that I love You. You gotta know that I need You.

Gm7(4)   **F2/A**   **B♭2(no3)**
God of wisdom and love, settle down from above.
        Csus   **Gm7(4)**
Give us all a taste of what Your Holy Spirit can do.
              F2/A   **B♭2(no3)**
Time and time again we've betrayed, but our debt's already been paid.
            Csus
And all that leaves me wanting is to live for You, God.

              D♭   **E♭**
And when the world crashes down around me,
             F   **Am/E**
I know You'll be there to pull me out from the rubble.
       B♭m7   **Gm7(♭5)**
When my enemy surrounds and I call on Your name,
        F   **Am7/E**   **B♭2**
You'll be there to deliver me from my troubled   soul.

Gm7(4)   F2/A   B♭2(no3)   Csus   F   B♭maj9   Dm7   B♭2   C

C/E   Dm   Dm/C   D♭   E♭   Am/E   B♭m7   Gm7(♭5)   Am7/E

Give It All Away

**Words and Music by
AARON SHUST**

D/F♯   **C/E**   **G/D**   **D/F♯**
Search my heart, search my mind, search my soul.
D2/F♯   **C/E**   **G/D**   **D/F♯**
Make me clean, make me new, make me whole.

      C2/E   **C2(no3)**   **G**   **D/F♯**
All of my plans, all of my dreams, I lay them down before Your feet.
      C2/E   **C2(no3)**   **G**   **D/F♯**
All of my time, all that was mine, I now submit to Your design,
      Am7   **G/B**   **C2**   **D**   **G2(no3)**
'Cause You are the One and only One who dared to give it all away for me.
      Bm7/F♯   **F2**   **C/E**
You dared to give it all away for me.

D/F♯   **C/E**   **G/D**   **D/F♯**
You are my strength. You are my God. You are my King.
D2/F♯   **C/E**   **G/D**   **D/F♯**
You make me laugh. You make me dance. You make me sing.

C2/E   **G**   **Bm7/F♯**   **G/F**   **C2/E**
Gave it all away. Everything inside, everything outside, I give it all away.
G   **Bm7/F♯**   **G/F**   **C2/E**
You never change, but You rearrange my heart more everyday.

      Am7   **G/B**   **C2**   **D**
'Cause You are the One who can make my life complete.
      Am7   **G/B**   **C2**   **D**
You are the One who can give light to my feet.
      Am7   **G/B**   **C2**   **D**   **G**
You are the One and only One who dared to give it all away for me.
      Bm7/F♯   **Gsus/F**   **Cmaj7/E**   **G**
You dared to give it all away for me. You dared to give it all away.
      Bm7/F♯   **Gsus/F**   **Cmaj7/E**   **D/F♯**
You gave it all away for me. You gave it all away for me.
      C2/E   **G**   **D**
Search my heart, search my mind, search my soul.

D/F♯   C/E   G/D   D2/F♯   C2/E   C2(no3)   G   Am7   G/B   C2   D   G2(no3)   Bm7/F♯   F2   G/F   Gsus/F   Cmaj7/E

Change the Way

**Words and Music by
AARON SHUST**

E   E/D#   C#m9   Bsus   A2(no3)
King of all the universe,   we love You.

      C#m   B7sus   E   E/D#
And we come to You now   asking for Your healing touch.

C#m9   Bsus   A2(no3)   C#m   B7sus
    We need You this very hour.

D   A/C#   E   B/D# B
  Would You help us comprehend what it means to worship You?

D   A/C#   F   Esus
  'Cause we're blinded by our circumstance. Heal our eyes today.

N.C.   A   F#m
May we know Your love; feel it course through our veins,

             D   F#m   E
Encircling our hearts and embracing our souls.

             A   F#m
We need Your love and grace to remain,

             D   Esus   E   D2(no3)
To rearrange our hearts,   and change the way we praise.

E   E/D#   C#m9   Bsus   A2(no3)
Son of God who took my place,   we thank You.

      C#m   B7sus   E   E/D#
And may we realize You've made us righteous in His sight.

    C#m9   Bsus   A2(no3) C#m   B7sus
You took our wrongs and made them right. We owe You   all of our lives.

F#m   E   D
Love me, Father, for I am Your son. (I am Your daughter).

F#m   E   D   F   G
Love me, Father, for I am Your son. (I am Your daughter).

E   E/D#   C#m9   Bsus   A2(no3)   C#m   B7sus   D   A/C#   B/D#   B   F   Esus   A   F#m   D2(no3)   G

My Savior, My God

Words and Music by
AARON SHUST
and DOROTHY GREENWELL

     D   **Bm**

I am not skilled to understand what God has willed, what God has planned.

     A   **D**

I only know at His right hand stands One who is my Savior.

     D   **Bm**

I take Him at His word and deed. Christ died to save me: this I read.

     Asus   **D**

And in my heart I find a need of Him to be my Savior.

          G   **D**

That He would leave His place on high and come for sinful man to die.

          Asus   **D**

You count it strange, so once did I before I knew my Savior.

   Bm   **G**   **D**   **A**

My Savior loves. My Savior lives. My Savior's always there for me.

   Bm   **G**   **D**   **A**

My God, He was. My God, He is. My God is always gonna be.

   Bm   **G**   **D**   **A**

My Savior loves. My Savior lives. My Savior's always there for me.

   Bm   **G**   **D**   **A**

My God, He was. My God, He is. My God is always gonna be.

     D   **Bm**

Yes, living, dying: let me bring my strength, my solace from this spring:

     Asus   **D**

That He who lives to be my King once died to be my Savior.

D   Bm   A   Asus   G

Stand to Praise (Psalm 117)

Words and Music by
AARON SHUST

Am   **F2**   **C**   **G/B**
Everybody,   praise the Lord, praise the Lord.
     Am   **F2**   **G**
And every nation,   applaud His name.
Am   **F2**   **C**   **G/B**
Everybody,   praise the Lord, praise the Lord.
     Am   **F2**   **G**
And every nation,   applaud His name.

     F   **C/E**
For great is His love toward us. The faithfulness of the Lord endures.
     Dm7   **G**
The faithfulness of the Lord endures forever.

                    C   **Am**
We stand to praise You, Lord. We stand to praise You, Lord.
                    Gsus   **F(no3)**
We stand to praise You, Lord. We stand to praise You, Lord.

Dm7   **F**   **C**   **G/B**
     Be at rest once more, my soul, for the Lord has been good to You.
Dm7   **F**   **C G/B**
     Be at rest once more, oh my soul.
Dm7   **F**   **C**   **G/B**
     Be at rest once more, my soul, for the Lord has been good to You.
B♭2(no3)   **C(no3)**
     Be at rest once more.   Be at rest once more.

                    D   **Bm**
We stand to praise You, Lord. We stand to praise You, Lord.
                    Asus   **G(no3)   D(no3)**
We stand to praise You, Lord. We stand to praise You, Lord.

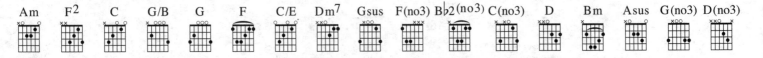

Am   F2   C   G/B   G   F   C/E   Dm7   Gsus   F(no3)   B♭2(no3)   C(no3)   D   Bm   Asus   G(no3)   D(no3)

In Your Name

Words and Music by
AARON SHUST

D   **C2**   **D**
In Your name You took the blind man, and You gave him back his sight.

                C2   **D**
In Your name You took the dead man, and You brought Him back to life.

                C2   **D**
In Your name You took this prisoner, and You opened up the doors,

                C2
And I will sing before Your throne forevermore.

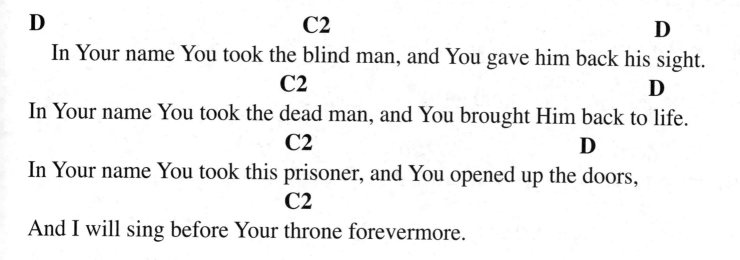

One Day

Words and Music by
AARON SHUST and DAN HANNON

G(no3)   **D**   **C**
One day, I will leave this body, and I will get a perfect one.

G **D**   **C**
That day, I will see His glory shining like the noonday sun.

G **D**   **C**   **G**
One day, I'll take a walk with Jesus. He might explain the mysteries of life.

    D   **C**
Some say, "I just can't believe it." But I know that one day

          A(no3)   **G/B**
We (I) will gather at the Crystal Throne. All these years: we're finally home.

C   **D**
I can actually see His face, and all I can do is say,

G   **D**   **Em**   **D**   **C**
Holy, Holy is the Lord Almighty, who was and is   and is to come.

    G   **D**
We lay our crowns before You, every heart and soul adore You,

    Em   **D**   **C**
The God of gods,   Almighty One.

G(no3)   **D**   **C**
One day, death will be abolished, and sin will have its mastery no more.

G **D**   **C**
And I know that we will be astonished at all that our Creator has in store.

G **D**   **C**   **G**
One day we will meet our Savior, and He will give each one of us a stone

    D   **C**
Engraved with our names upon it: "Known by God alone."

Em   **D**   **C**   **Em**   **D** **C**   **G** **F** **G**
King of kings,   God's only Son. The Lord of lords,   salvation done!

G(no3)	D	C	G	A(no3)	G/B	Em	F